Prolegomena to the Study of Old Welsh Poetry

By

Edward Anwyl

First published in 1903

Published by Left of Brain Books

Copyright © 2023 Left of Brain Books

ISBN 978-1-396-32514-4

First Edition

All rights reserved. No part of this publication may be reproduced, distributed, or transmitted in any form or by any means, including photocopying, recording, or other electronic or mechanical methods, without the prior written permission of the publisher, except in the case of brief quotations permitted by copyright law. Left of Brain Books is a division of Left Of Brain Onboarding Pty Ltd.

PUBLISHER'S PREFACE

About the Book

"Since the later Middle Ages, the traditional Welsh poetic metres in strict verse consist of twenty four different metrical forms written in cynghanedd.

An awdl is a form of long poem, similar to the ode. The most popular metrical forms are the Cywydd, of 14th century origin, and the several versions of the Englyn, a concise and allusive verse form similar to the Greek epigram and the Japanese haiku and as old as Welsh literature itself."

(Quote from wikipedia.org)

About the Author

Edward Anwyl (1866 - 1914)

"Sir Edward Anwyl (August 5, 1866 – August 8, 1914), was a Welsh academic, specializing in the Celtic languages.

Anwyl was born in Chester, England, and educated at the King's School, Chester. He went on to study at Oriel College, Oxford, and Mansfield College, Oxford. In 1892 he became Professor of Welsh at the University of Wales, Aberystwyth, and was later appointed Professor of Comparative Philology. He was knighted in 1911. In 1913, he became Principal of the newly-founded. Monmouthshire Training College at Caerleon."

(Quote from wikipedia.org)

CONTENTS

PUBLISHER'S PREFACE
    PROLEGOMENA TO THE STUDY OF OLD WELSH POETRY............. 1

PROLEGOMENA TO THE STUDY OF OLD WELSH POETRY

IT will probably be readily admitted by those acquainted with Celtic studies that the most difficult subject in the sphere of Welsh literature is the critical interpretation and translation of the oldest Welsh poetry, and this is a problem of interest not only to Welshmen, but to a wider circle, as part of the larger question of the origins of the vernacular literature of Western Europe. The difficulty referred to is due in no small degree to the obsolete character of the vocabulary, but it is also due to the difficulty of correcting the text on the one hand, and that of classifying and interpreting the allusions to persons and places on the other. Much work has been done by students of Celtic in these various directions, but, in the absence of some short introductory treatment, the novice often fails to appreciate the problems for solution, and the significance of the various scattered pieces of research that are intended as answers to them. Further, the progress of these studies has been hampered in the past by an inadequate study of the historical grammar of the Welsh language, and of the peculiarities of the earlier syntactical constructions as distinguished from those of later times. The great work of Zeuss, though of abiding value, needs supplementing, especially on the poetical side of old Welsh grammar.

The present writer has given a preliminary statistical account of several of the older verbal forms in an Appendix to Welshmen, by the Rev. T. Stephens, but it would be well if all the grammatical forms could be similarly tabulated. Another important line of research which is indispensable to the elucidation of the older poetry, is a close study of the older prose remains of Welsh in order to determine, if possible, their structure, literary affinities, and topographical relations. The present writer has also contributed a preliminary discussion of some of these points, especially in relation to the 'Four Branches of the Mabinogi', to the Zeitschrift für Celtische Philologie. The present paper is a development of the same study, and is the outcome of a consideration of the inter-relations of the oldest prose and poetic writings of the Welsh people.

in dealing with these subjects, again, it has to be borne in mind that, whatever may be the origins of these forms of literature, they come to us in what may be termed a mediaeval dress. just as the 'Four Branches of the Mabinogi' in their present form reflect the ideas of the Feudal System, so, too, many of the poems attributed to Taliesin and others reflect the monastic studies of the Middle Ages. Hence, in order to elucidate them, it is not necessary merely to guess at the underlying fragments of ancient mythology and legend, but also to study the medium through which these are presented. It is necessary, also, to form some idea of that conception of poetry and of the poet which made them possible. Celtic studies are here in special need of correlation on the literary side with researchers into the origins and early developments of the other literatures of Western Europe.

Again, apart from the comparison of Irish and Welsh literature, it is important that, as far as possible, the various stories commonly called 'Mabinogion', the older body of poetry, Gildas, the chronicle called 'Nennius' in its various recensions, the lives of the Welsh saints, and Geoffrey of Monmouth's History of the Kings of Britain, should be studied together. Along with these should also be closely investigated the oldest genealogies. These investigations may give us a clue to the families from whose spheres of influence portions of the older literature emanated, the districts where they were originally evolved, or to which they were transferred, and the probable literary centres of the ancient Welsh. Already very valuable and suggestive work in this direction has been done by Professor Zimmer in his Nennius Vindicatus, whereby he has brought into view the probable existence of old British or Welsh centres of literary activity in the North at Dumbarton or Carlisle, in Gwynedd, and in the Builth district.

In dealing with the old stories and old poems of Wales it is important to discover, wherever possible, the motives that appear to have led to their formation and development. It is from this point of view that the genealogies deserve careful study, in order to see what compositions may conceivably owe their origin to family or ecclesiastical pride. In the elucidation of the old genealogies a great debt of gratitude is due especially to Mr Egerton Phillimore and Mr Anscombe. A single name may at times prove an invaluable clue in these intricate and delicate researches.

The body of Welsh poetry here dealt with is commonly known as that of 'The Four Ancient Books of Wales', being The Black Book of Carmarthen, The Book of Aneurin, The Book of Taliesin, and The Red Book of Hergest. The interrelations of most of the poems contained in Skene's edition are sufficiently clear to reveal the fact that they represent in many respects a common tradition; nor does it require much research to show that, within the collection as a whole, there are various strata, which may often be distinguished with respect to their place of origin and their time of composition. The historical allusions, for example, of the 'Hoianau' poem (contained in the Black Book of Carmarthen) make it clear that it belongs to the twelfth century; while the orthography of 'Gorchan Maelderw' in the Book of Aneurin makes it quite clear that that poem, together with the analogous parts of the 'Gododdin', is earlier, at any rate, than the Book of Llandav. Again, the occasional lapses into an older mode of spelling, as in Poem xxiii of the Book of Taliesin, called 'Trawsganu Kynan Garwyn m. Brochwel Ysgythrog', where we have trefbret for trefret, pympðnt for pymhðnt, dymet for dyuet, suggest that the poem was copied from a manuscript in which the spelling was uniformly of an older type. Again, the reference in l. 885 of the 'Gododdin' to the death of Dyvynwal Vrych (Donald Brec), who died in 642, shows that the line, at any rate in the form there found, is subsequent to that date. Similarly, in l. 934 of the same poem, the reference to Gynt (= gentes, i.e. the Scandinavians) shows that, at least in that form, the line is subsequent to the Scandinavian incursions. We know, too, from the existence of a verse of the same series in an eleventh century MS. of St Augustine's 'De Trinitate', which is in the Library of Corpus Christi College, Cambridge, that verses of this same series of stanzas were known at that time. We have another instance in the Book of Taliesin. Even if we had no other reasons for forming that opinion, the existence of a reference to Bede in poem xvi, l. 38, would be a proof that the poem containing the reference was later than his time, that is, unless the line or the reference was interpolated. Again reverting to the 'Gododdin', the references to Elfin (l. 376) and to Beli (in l. 385) make it suspicious that they refer by an anachronism to Elfin, King of Alclud (Dumbarton), who died in 722 A.D., and to Beli his son. If this be so, then the other verses in praise of Eithinyn, such as those beginning 'Kywyrein ketwyr kywrennin' and those of corresponding characteristics, must have been written, at least, during the lifetime of Beli, the son. Moreover, it is obvious from the rhyme alone that all the old poems were composed after the old declensional and conjugational endings had been entirely lost.

If, again, we consider topographical allusions, we note that the numerous references to places in Powys and the neighbouring parts of England in the so-called 'Llywarch Hen' poems, make it highly probable that we have here a body of poetry which, in its nucleus and its imitators, flourished in the literary centres of Powys. A few allusions, such as those to Llyn Geirionydd, Nant Ffrancon, and Dyganhwy, in some of the Taliesin poems, create a presumption that the poet who wrote them was not unconnected either with the court of Gwynedd or with some Carnarvonshire or Anglesey monastery. We are tempted also to suspect that the body of old poetry, which forms the nucleus of the Book of Taliesin and the similar poetry of the Book of Aneurin, was either itself preserved in Dyganhwy, Bangor Deiniol, Bangor Seiriol, or Clynnog, or was based on some annals, containing references to events in the North, which we do not now fully possess. The reference in the Welsh Laws to the preservation of 'Breiniau Gwyr Arfon' by Bangor Deiniol and Bangor Beuno makes it not improbable that, in these and kindred monasteries, there were preserved brief annals and records, which afforded material to the bards and monks. There is extant in the Welsh Laws an interesting specimen of such a record, giving an account of the relations between the men of Arfon and the men of Strathclyde in the time of Rhun, son of Maelgwn Gwynedd. These brief annals were probably in close relation to the genealogies of the ruling families, and these families in the Cunedda districts, as well as those of other 'men of the North', may in some cases, owing to intermarriage, have comprised the names of some of the earlier inhabitants.

Professor Zimmer has suggested in his Nennius Vindicatus that in the original work of Nennius and in the North Wales recension, older annals from the North have played a part, notably in the account of the struggles between the Britons of the North and the men of Deira and Bernicia; it is highly probable, too, that chronicles of similar type have supplied the personal and local names which have been incorporated in the poems of the Four Ancient Books. As we shall see presently, these poems are not merely historical in character: they are an attempt at artistic treatment of historical themes which would be of special interest to certain Welsh families.

It is probably in brief annals such as these, too, combined with oral narrative, that we are to look for the materials which have been combined into the form of triads. These triads have obvious points of contact with the old poetry on the one hand, and with the prose narratives on the other. These chronicles need not by any means have belonged in all cases to the North; some of them may equally well have been evolved in the courts or in the leading monasteries of Gwynedd, Powys, Gwent and Dyfed, or even in the smaller territories of local dynasties. It is not improbable, too, that the pedigrees and the chronicles associated with them were the channels through which the names of ancient gods and goddesses, from whom certain families claimed descent, passed into later legend in association with historical names, as we find them for example in the 'Four Branches of the Mabinogi'.

The identification of the Northern localities of the old poetry has been ably prosecuted by Mr Skene, Mr Egerton Phillimore and others, but many names are still unidentified. Nor do Mr Skene's identifications in all cases carry conviction. In spite of his valuable service in bringing into prominence the Northern local background of many of the poems, he has often been too hasty in identifying place-names owing to a superficial similarity of sound. The great merit of his work consists in the fact that it enables us to realize dimly how long the descendants of 'Gwyr y Gogledd' regarded themselves, while in Wales and of Wales, as belonging to a larger Wales and to Britain as a whole, regarded not in mere isolation but as a part of the civilized world of the Roman Empire. It was probably this underlying and unsuppressed imperial instinct that made them dwell with evident delight on such imperial figures as Macsen, Helen and Arthur. The Welsh narratives scarcely ever confine the scenes of the exploits of their secular or ecclesiastical heroes to Wales, and the Welsh ruling families long regarded themselves as the survivors of Roman civilization. The after-glow of the Roman Empire long lingered in Britain. Evidence of the impression which Rome and the Latin tongue had made on Wales is afforded, not only by the number and quality of Latin words in Welsh, by the frequency of Latin names, but also by the attempts of Welshmen in remote corners of Wales to write the inscriptions of tomb-stones in Latin, in spite of their manifest ignorance of Latin spelling and grammar. There were probably men in Wales over a thousand years ago who expected a speedy end to the Welsh language.

in dealing with the early literature of Wales it is well to remember that ecclesiastical documents such as the Lives of the Welsh Saints, and more secular documents such as the Mabinogion, should be studied together. The ruling families of the monasteries and the ruling families of the courts were most closely related, and it is difficult, if not impossible, to separate the ecclesiastical literary centres of early times from the secular. In both these types of centres there was an equal pride in the exploits of the ancient families to which the saints and the ruling dynasties belonged, and the perpetuation in song of the exploits of the 'Men of the North' and others would be as natural for a monastic as for a courtly bard.

No one who studies early Welsh history and literature can fail to remark the prominence of families and traditions from the North in post-Roman times. It is not improbable that when Cunedda came into Wales from Manaw Gododdin, he came by the express invitation of the Brythons, who found themselves in need of experienced military support against the incursions of

Irishmen from the West and the recrudescence of activity on the part of the mixed Goidelic and pre-Celtic population. After the withdrawal of the Roman fleets from the British seas, Britain was exposed to inroads of Irish pirates from the West as well as of Teutonic pirates from the East, alike eager for the plunder of one of the finest provinces of the Roman Empire. Except in the North, Britain at the time of the departure of the Romans was, from all indications, in a state of profound peace and quiet civilization. Hence the Brythons of Wales, in the face of invasion from the West, naturally turned for aid to the experienced military Brythons of the North, and gratefully accepted their continuance at the head of affairs in Wales. Though the Elegy on Cunedda Wledig in the Book of Taliesin (poem xlvi) is undoubtedly much later than his time, as is shown, for example, in the rhymes Cunedaf and gðynaf, yet it may possibly be modelled on some older composition, or may be based on some annalistic document. In dealing with the early vernacular literature of Wales we have always to bear in mind its aristocratic character, and its relation to the ideas and traditions of the ruling families, who long preserved their interest in the district from which their fathers had come.

Behind the heroic traditions of the Northern families, however, we are driven, by the parallel study of the old poems and the Mabinogion, to consider whether some of the traditions of still older families may not have survived, linked it may be with their genealogies. Through intermarriage with the older strata of the population the men of the North would enter into the inheritance of these legends, which would in course of time be incorporated with theirs, though still regarded as belonging to an older epoch. It is possibly this distinction that is perpetuated in the apparently scrupulous care taken in the 'Four Branches of the Mabinogi' and, indeed, throughout the Mabinogion, to draw clear lines of demarcation between the various legendary periods, in accordance with a tendency discernible in Nennius and even in Geoffrey, in spite of his anachronisms. It looks as if there was a kind of traditional framework, into which the narrative of early British events was supposed to fit. The literary men of the courts and of the monasteries were doubtless equally assiduous in filling in this framework with all kinds of local stories, now attributed to this hero, now to that, largely derived from the never-failing staple of aetiological myth. Nor must we forget the possibility that even the men of the North may have brought with them some such tales as, for example, stories of Manawyd or Manawyddan, the eponymous hero of Manaw Gododdin, or that places in Wales, according to the wont of settlers, may have been renamed after places in the North or after the heroes of the Northern legends. The difficulty of tracing the topographical relations of these legends is increased when we remember that the geography of legends tends to expand with the expansion of men's ideas and territorial interests, a tendency of which we have a conspicuous example in the Arthurian geography of Geoffrey of Monmouth. It is not improbable that this phenomenon is an important feature even of the 'Four Branches of the Mabinogi' as we have them in their present form.

Another point which should always be borne in mind in dealing with Welsh as well as other legends is, that to historical names non-historical stories may become attached, and that the stories so attached may be far more ancient than the names. In dealing with the old stories of Wales, whether in prose or poetry, it would be well to reduce them to their simplest terms, thus bringing to view their typical plots. If this were systematically done with the stories of the other branches of the Celtic family, and, indeed, over a wider area, it would be easy to institute a kind of synoptic comparison of these plots. The writer is well aware how much admirable work has already been done in this direction by distinguished students of Celtic, such as Principal Rhys, and other students of folklore, but it would nevertheless be a great convenience if the various types of stories could be succinctly tabulated for the purpose of comparison, according to their characteristic plots, expressed in the briefest possible terms. Such a concise treatment would be of great value in comparing the ancient stories of Wales with those, for instance, of Ireland.

If we now turn to the older poetry of Wales, we see that much of it reflects the period of heroic struggle against the English. This is the case in the Book of Aneurin, in a few poems of the Book of Taliesin, in one or two poems (notably that in praise of Geraint) in the Black Book of Carmarthen, and in some of the Llywarch Hen poems of the Red Book of Hergest. While the Book of Aneurin and the poems of the Book of Taliesin mainly commemorate the Northern struggles against the men of Deira and Bernicia, those of the Red Book of Hergest and the corresponding portions of the Black Book of Carmarthen commemorate the struggle in the Severn Valley and the adjacent districts. Some of the heroes of the conflict in both cases belong to the same cycle, and, whatever may be the age of the actual compositions as we have them, they are probably based on older annals and lists of famous battles, but they are unfortunately much too vague to supply us with definite historical information. It must be remembered, too, that a critical analysis of the 'Gododdin' shews it not to be one poem, but to be composed of portions of several poems. An analysis of the 'Gododdin' (which itself contains repetitions) side by side with 'Gorchan Maelderw' shews clearly that these two poems consist of more or less identical portions of one and the same series of poems. In the greater part of the 'Gododdin' and the Gorchanau of the Book of Aneurin ('Gorchan Tutvwlch', 'Gorchan Adebon', 'Gorchan Cynvelyn' and 'Gorchan Maelderw') the copyist changed the orthography of the MS. from which he was copying into that of the early part of the thirteenth century, but, fortunately, he has, here and there, been careless in the performance of this task, and, in a large part of 'Gorchan Maelderw' he has left the spelling of the MS. before him practically unaltered, thus revealing a part of the poem in its pre-Norman dress, and even in a form which comes very near to that of the glosses of the eighth and ninth centuries. It is evident, too, that what was here copied was merely a string of fragments, so that the original poems from which they are taken, and which were the originals also of the larger fragments that are now in the 'Gododdin', were older still, though how much older it would be difficult to say. It is interesting to note that 'Gorchan Maelderw' is attributed in the MS. to Taliesin, whereas the very same portions in the 'Gododdin' are attributed in the same manuscript to Aneurin. It should also be observed that in 'Gorchan Maelderw' and in certain portions of the latter half of the 'Gododdin', the account of the battle of Catraeth, with which the poem deals, differs somewhat from that of the earlier portion. In 'Gorchan Maelderw' and its cognate portions of the 'Gododdin', all the Britons are represented as being killed, except one, and he appears to be Cynon ab Clydno Eiddin. In the earlier portion of the 'Gododdin' those who are represented as escaping out of the general slaughter are said to be Cynon, together with 'deu gatki aeron' (Kyndilic and Kynan) and Aneurin, into whose mouth the narrative of the battle and the praises of the warriors (living and dead) who fought at the battle, are put. Moreover, Aneurin, where he is represented as escaping, is so represented in two ways: one way is that after being wounded ('om gwaetffreu') he escapes through the power of his song; the other, where he is represented as being freed from an underground dungeon by Ceneu son of Llywarch. It is clear from both the 'Gododdin' and 'Gorchan Maelderw' that the leading theme of these two poems is the praise of Cynon ab Clydno Eiddin, probably a much more important personage in early Welsh history and legend than his present fame might lead us to suspect. Of his early fame it may be noted that there is some reflection in Owain and Luned. Some indication, too, of this earlier prominence is given by the number of Englynion on him in 'Englynion y Beddau'. We should probably not be far wrong in regarding this group of poems as being one section of the poetry composed in honour of the Coel family (Coeling) and especially the 'Cynverching' (family of Cynvarch) branch of that stock, the branch to which Urien Rheged belonged. It should be borne in mind that it was the duty of a family bard not merely to glorify the living, but also to preserve and to enhance the fame of the dead ancestors of his living patrons, and this he could hardly do better than by amplifying and embellishing in verse the chronicles of the battles in which they showed their prowess. Owing to the close relationship, too, between the families of the Welsh saints and those of the princes, the above-mentioned motive would operate even among the monastic bards. The importance of the Coel family is well illustrated in a statement made in 'Bonedd Gwyr y Gogledd' (Hengwrt MS. 536). 'Trychan cledyf kynuerchyn a ttrychan ysgðyt kynnðdyon a ttrychan wayð coeling pa neges bynhac yd elynt iddi yn duun. Nyt amethei (hon) honno.'

As the 'Gododdin' is now given in the Book of Aneurin, the verses have, in several cases, been transposed from their original order, so that what we now have are disjecta membra; and in some places there appear to be irrelevant interpolations. The earlier part of the 'Gododdin' appears to have affinities with 'Gorchan Tutvwlch'; for, in both, Tutvwlch and Kyfwlch are jointly commemorated along with Cynon. 'Gorchan Cynfelyn', which mentions Eithinyn, a 'Gododdin' hero, differs from 'Gorchan Maelderw' in referring to the escape of three men from Catraeth, one of whom is Cynon, and the other two Cadreith and Catleu o gatnant, together with Aneurin, who, after being wounded, is ransomed, by the sons of Coel (reading meib) for pure gold, steel and silver. The Cynfelyn here commemorated is probably Cynfelyn Drwsgl, the brother of Cynon ab Clydno Eiddin. Possibly the chief centres from which these poems emanated were Dyganhwy, Bangor Seiriol (in Anglesey, the land of Caw's descendants), Bangor Deiniol, Bangor Beuno (not far from which was a Cefn Clutno) and Llanbadarn. The latter centre is here mentioned because one of the 'Englynion y Beddau' represents Cynon ab Clydno Eiddin as having been buried there. Cor Seiriol in Penmon and Cor Beuno in Clynnog both appear to have acquired a high reputation for their learning. Elaeth Frenin ab Meyrig (the supposed author of 'Kygogion Elaeth' in the Black Book of Carmarthen) was a monk at Bangor Seiriol, and Nidan ab Gwrfyw ab Pasgen ab Urien Rheged is said to have been some time an abbot there. It may well be that it is to the old monastic schools, even more than to the courts of the princes, that we are to look in the early period for the development of Welsh literature, and it is not impossible, were more known of these schools, that they were the direct successors of still earlier teachers. In dealing with the earlier poetry it should not be forgotten that even the 'Gododdin' contains numerous religious allusions.

The poem of the Book of Aneurin called 'Gorchan Maelderw' is of great interest, because, in one of the portions of it written in an archaic orthography, the name of Arthur unmistakably occurs in the words 'bei ef Arthur' (even if he were Arthur). These words suggest that even then, within the cycle of the Catraeth poems, Arthur's praise and fame were great. Indeed, from every point of view the indications (as in the Black Book poems) point to the conclusion that, within the circle of traditions connected with the struggle against the English, Arthur, though rarely mentioned, was throughout a commanding figure.

Let us now turn for a moment to poems of another series. The early poetry of Powys, which is attributed to Llywarch Hen, bases its chief claim to antiquity on the undoubted fact that several of the poems are similar in form to some 'englynion' of the ninth century, which are found in the Juvencus Codex of the Cambridge University Library. Some of these poems, such as those in praise of Geraint ab Erbin, are also found in the Black Book of Carmarthen. Hence, it may be concluded that the nucleus of this poetry formed part of that heroic tradition which commemorated the leaders of the struggle against the English in parts of the Severn Valley, being, in fact, the East Wales analogue of the tradition of the struggle in the North found in the 'Gododdin' and kindred poems. It is of interest to observe that in the poems of both series Arthur appears as a prominent figure. The poems of the Powys and Severn struggles appear to have as their prose counterpart a chronicle such as that which Professor Zimmer in his Nennius Vindicatus has shewn to underlie the Builth recension of Nennius, while the poems of the 'Gododdin' series appear to have closer affinities with the chronicles which underlie the Venedotian recension. From one courtly or monastic literary centre to another the story of Arthur and his associated companions, such as Cai, Bedwyr, Owain ab Urien, Caradog Vreichvras, Cynon ab Clydno Eiddin, seems to have spread through the Wye and Severn Valleys, and notably the Usk Valley (until Caerleon on Usk became a great Arthurian locality) and even much further afield. Nennius already speaks of Arthur, at Carn Cabal near Builth, hunting the 'Porcus Troyt', and of the grave of Arthur's son in Erging. We know, too, from Giraldus Cambrensis, that the highest point of the Breconshire Beacons was known in his time as Kadeir Arthur, the throne of Arthur.

The bulk of the Llywarch Hen poetry, as we have it in the Red Book of Hergest, is marked by a meditative pathos, and it is to this pathos that it owes much of its charm. These poems appear to have been written by someone acquainted with the traditional story of Llywarch Hen and with the narrative of the struggle of the Welsh against the English around Pengwern. The poet's favourite vein of reflection is over the departure of the brilliance and joy of the past. In this vein he represents Llywarch Hen as mourning over the loss of youth with its joy and vigour, over the death of his children, over the loss of his former lords, Urien and Cynddylan, and also over the former glories of the ancient palaces of Pengwern and the neighbourhood. As compared with the spirit of the 'Gododdin' and kindred poetry, it may be said that the Llywarch Hen compositions appeal to the sense of pathos and of contrast in a broader and more catholic way. In both types there is a strong appeal to the sense of contrast, but in the 'Gododdin' the contrast depicted is between the confident gaiety and exuberant hilarity which preceded the battle of Catraeth, and the disastrous event of the contest, between the host that went to battle and the fragment of it that returned. In the Llywarch Hen poetry the contrast is between the glory of the past and the ruin of the present. Neither group of poems is the bare unreflecting primitive poetry of narrative: it is a poetry which seeks to appeal to minds thoroughly alive to the pathos and tragedy of life as exemplified in the events and the results of the great struggle of the Britons.' It is the 'lacrimae rerum' in this body of poetry that give it an abiding interest. What influence (if any) the study of Vergil, the universal school book of the Roman Empire and of the Middle Ages, may have had in giving this direction of pathos to Welsh poetry it is now impossible to say.

The poetry with which we have hitherto dealt, though not without religious allusions, is in the main of a humanistic character, but in addition to these poems the body of poetry now under consideration comprises a number of poems that are primarily religious, and others which contain a strong tincture of mediaeval theology combined with other elements. The most curious poetry of the latter type is that mainly, though not exclusively, found in the Book of Taliesin, where theology, mediaeval natural history and various legends are presented together through a medium which reveals a very curious conception of the poetic art. In this body of poetry, some of which contains materials derived from the Northern traditional stock, the poet is depicted not as mourning over the disastrous battles of the past or lamenting the departed greatness of his race, so much as rising supernaturally above human limitations of time and place, and reviewing the famous events of the heroic and legendary past, in which he himself is represented as having been present. This idea is partly the result of the thought that the materials of the body had been in existence from time immemorial, partly a development from the favourite mediaeval idea of metamorphosis, the latter idea being part and parcel of the universal magical conceptions of the time. The composer of the poems, in recounting his supposed past experiences, seems to have quarried in some ancient chronicles containing lists of the battles of Urien Rheged and others, and of the localities in which they were fought. Nor is it unlikely that some older lines were bodily adopted and incorporated from ancient heroic Poems and elegies. These old traditions appear to have had a special charm for some of the poets of the Book of Taliesin, and they would seem to have been particularly fond of traditions and legends which flourished in Anglesey and Carnarvonshire. The references to Geirionydd and Nant Ffrancon appear to indicate the neighbourhood of the Conwy valley and Dyganhwy as one of the poets' gathering-ground of legend. To this district we may perhaps link the Hiraethog district and the valley of the Dyfrdwy beyond. From the Carnarvonshire side the poet probably obtained a stock of Don and Beli legends, from Dyganhwy and the neighbourhood the local legends of Taliesin, while from the Hiraethog and the Dee district came the legends of Bran and Branwen, with the topographical associations of which I have dealt in my articles on the 'Four Branches of the Mabinogi' in the Zeitschrift für Celtische Philologie. The Branwen legend was also associated with Merionethshire and Anglesey, and the legend of Pryderi with Merionethshire. In the 'Four Branches of the Mabinogi' it may be noted that the topographical associations of the Don family are mainly with the West side of Carnarvonshire. The district of the Conwy valley and the nearest parts of Anglesey and Carnarvonshire probably felt a certain local interest in Seithennin, the father of St Tudno, in Urien Rheged (the ancestor of Grwst of Llanrwst and of Nidan, at one time head of the monastery of Penmon), in Lleenawg, from whose name Castell Lleiniog on the Anglesey side of the Menai Straits seems to be called, in Dona of Llanddona, a descendant of Brochwel Ysgythrog, in Maelgwn Gwynedd, whose court was at Dyganhwy and possibly in Arthur, if the name Bwrdd Arthur is ancient. The composer of many of these Taliesin poems is not content, however, to build merely on a basis of traditional and local legend, but interweaves his fantastic imaginings into a tissue of mediaeval natural philosophy, largely derived from the stock manuals of the dark ages, the works of Isidore of Seville and Bede, who were the chief successors of the encyclopaedists Martianus Capella and Cassiodorus. The poet expresses his respect for Bede in the line

Nyt ðy dyðeit geu llyfreu beda.

i.e., The books of Bede do not speak falsehood.

The conception of a poet revealed in many of these poems seems very strange to us at the present day, but it bears a very strong resemblance to the mediaeval conception of Vergil (known in mediaeval Welsh as 'Fferyll', and mentioned under that name in one of the Taliesin poems). The magical connotation of the name 'Fferyll' may be seen from the fact that it is the origin of the Welsh 'fferyllydd', chemist. According to the mediaeval conception of Vergil, as we see from Professor Comparetti's account of Vergil in the Middle Ages, he was not only a man of supreme learning, but was also endowed with super-human powers. Fortunately, owing to the general atmosphere of these poems, the bent of the composers towards natural history has preserved for us some interesting old Welsh terms, such as 'adfant', the upper world; 'difant' (whence 'difancoll'), the lower world; 'elfydd', the earth; 'annwfn', the under world, 'anghar', 'affwys' and 'affan', apparently of the same meaning. The latter may, however, be borrowed through Latin from Greek {greek afaués}; from Latin are certainly derived the terms 'aches', the flood tide; and 'reges', the ebb tide, from 'accessus' and 'recessus' respectively. How greatly interested the Britons were in the tides we see from several passages in the Book of Taliesin and the Black Book of Carmarthen, from the De Mirabilibus Britanniae, and from a treatise De Mirabilibus, formerly attributed to St Augustine, and now believed to be the work of a Briton. The term 'llafanad', formed by means of a Welsh ending -ad from 'llafan' (a parallel form of 'llafn', like mediaeval 'gauar' and 'gafyr'), which comes from Latin 'lamina', may be roughly translated 'element', but it probably reflected originally a conception of existence, whereby its various substances tended to form 'laminations' or layers. It may be noted, too, that the familiar terms of 'Macrocosm' and 'Microcosm' appear in these poems as 'Y Byt Mawr' and 'Y Byt Bychan'. The use of these and other terms suggests affinities between the medium of ideas through which the traditions and legends are presented, and an obscure type of philosophical doctrine which lived on as a kind of undergrowth in the Roman Empire and the Dark Ages, a body of doctrine believed by some to have had a share in the formation of the Jewish Kabbala. One of its best known representatives is the Poemander of Hermes Trismegistus.

It should be noted that in an interesting dialogue between the soul and the body found in the Black Book of Carmarthen, the Taliesin doctrine of 'Y saith llafanad' is put into the mouth of the body. In this account the body is formed by the meeting together of the seven 'laminations', of which fire, earth, wind, mist, flowers, are named, but the other two, water and air (see the Book of Taliesin, poem lv) are omitted, around the pure substance ('put').

This super-human conception of the poet shows itself, as we have seen in his attitude towards the past, but it is no less visible in his attitude towards the future. The prophetic powers of the poet come here especially into view. Here again we have an interesting point of contact with the mediaeval conception of Vergil as a prophet. In Wales, the role of the prophetic bard is that of prophesying to the remnants of the Britons ultimate victory over their enemies, under the leadership of some of the leaders of the past, notably, Cynan and Cadwaladr. These vaticinations were put sometimes into the mouth of Tallesin, sometimes into the mouth of Myrddin Wyllt. The earliest 'Myrddin' prophecy is that put into the mouth of Merlinus Ambrosius in Nennius, in a narrative which has evident affinities with that of 'Lludd and Llevelys'. This prophecy was afterwards developed by Geoffrey of Monmouth, and became extremely popular. In 1180 a commentary was written upon it by Alanus de Insulis, and in 1208 a translation of the prophecies was made into Icelandic. A version appeared also in French and became very popular. In 1379 an Italian translation was made which also attained popularity. In 1478 a German version was published, and in 1498 a version appeared in Spanish. It should be noted that the favourite Myrddin of Welsh poetry is Myrddin Wylltt, who is not associated with the Nennius story at all, but with

Rhydderch Hael and Gwenddoleu, as we see in the 'Hoianau' and 'Afallenau'.

As already stated, the framework of the Welsh Myrddin poems is the story of Myrddin Wyllt, as may be seen in the twelfth-century poems of the 'Afallenau' and 'Hoianau' of the Black Book of Carmarthen. In his madness after the Battle of Arderydd, Myrddin utters his prognostications as to the future of the Welsh people. His companion in his wanderings is a little pig, and we catch sight also of a lady who appears to stand in much the same relation to Myrddin as the Sibyl to Virgil in the legend of the Middle Ages. Her name is Chwimleian or Chwipleia, and she appears to be the same as Viviane of the Breton stories. In the Book of Taliesin, poem vi, called 'Arymes Prydein', is a Myrddin vaticination, as well as poem xlvii, which begins with the line

Dygogan awen dygobryssyn,

and poems i and liii. In the Red Book of Hergest (as given in Skene) the type in question is represented by poems xviii, xix, xx, xxi, as well as poems i and ii, 'Kyvoessi Myrdin a Gwendyd' and 'Gwasgargert Myrtin' respectively. Poems of a prophetic type long continued popular in England and in Wales. When we turn to distinctively religious poems and hymns there are many points of contact, as might have been expected, with the general trend of mediaeval thought, as seen, for example, in a collection like Mone's Latin Hymns of the Middle Ages. In the Black Book of Carmarthen we have in the first place a 'Dialogue between the Soul and the Body' (Skene, vol. ii, poems v, vi and vii). This poem ends with a description of the Day of Judgment on Mount Olivet, a favourite subject of mediaeval hymnology. Poem ix of the same manuscript is meant to be a warning to the wicked of his fate. In poems x, xi and xii, there are reflections of mediaeval theology. In poem xi, it is interesting to note the

Divine names Eloy and Adonay, probably taken from a list given by Isidore of Seville. In this poem, too, we have the names 'Paul ac Anhun' (Antony), which suggest the monastic atmosphere of the writer. Poem xiii gives some interesting non-scriptural stories about Job, Eve and the infant Christ. In poems xx and xxi we have compositions attributed to 'Elaeth' or 'Elaeth Frenin', who is said to have become a monk. Poem xxv is of similar type, while in xxvii there are references to Sanffreid (St Bridget), Gwosprid (St Osbert) and St Peter. The whole of this poem is a curious combination, in the style of the Llywarch Hen poetry, of a hymn with an account of the preparations for a journey. In poem xxix we have one of those Welsh mediaeval poems where religious emotion is blended with an enquiring interest in natural phenomena.

The Book of Taliesin also affords several specimens of religious poems of the above type, side by side with others which have a curious admixture of legend, natural history or magical imagination. In poem i (as printed in the Book of Taliesin) from l. 21 to the end there are clear indications of the religious milieu in which this type of poetry arose. Poem ii (162 lines) is called 'Marwnat Y Vil Veib', and reflects in its heavenly and earthly hierarchy the Pseudo-Dionysian theology which dominated the church of that time. The poem contains some curious scraps of Latin and of geography. Poem v (173 lines) is a description of the Day of Judgment and of the punishment of Christ's crucifiers. In poem xxii we have a meditation on the 'Plagues of Egypt' (Plaeu yr Eifft), while poem xxiv is an account of Moses' Rod (Llath Moesen). There is another poem (No. li) of the same cycle on the twelve tribes of Israel (Deudec tref yr Israel). Poem xxvi is a short poem on the Trinity, and xxix is of interest not only on account of its scriptural allusions, but also on account of its reference to Alexander the Great, a feature which indicates its affinity with poems xxvi and xxviii, and with the mediaeval

Alexander literature generally. This literature was especially popular in France and Ireland. Poem xli appears to refer to the cruelty of Erof (for Erodd = Herod); while poems lv and lvi, to which reference has already been made, are called 'Kanu y Byt Mawr' (the Macrocosm) and 'Kanu y Byt Bychan' (the Microcosm). These two latter poems are clearly based on the writings of Isidore of Seville, Bede and similar authors. Further researches into the books read in the monasteries in the early Middle Ages, such as may be seen for example in the Catalogues of the Ancient Libraries of Canterbury and Dover, will undoubtedly throw much light on the religious and other poems of the Four Ancient Books. Before these poems can be safely used for the purpose of comparative mythology it is necessary to elucidate the mediaeval medium through which they are presented, just as in the study of the 'Four Branches of the Mabinogi', and other old stories, it is important to bear in mind the re-casting which they have undergone to suit mediaeval ideas. In the mediaeval matrix of many of these poems, however, there are embedded many highly interesting portions of early legend, whose topographical affinities have now been ascertained with some measure of success. An important problem which remains is that of classifying these legends according to their various interrelations and affinities. In this work some help may be given by 'Englynion y Beddau' and other poems.

In dealing with the old poetry of Wales and its kindred literature it is well to keep apart the framework of persons, incidents and localities in which the stories are placed, and the essential features of the stories themselves. Stories far older than the framework may here as elsewhere have become attached in course of time to the historical names of Northern or Welsh native families, Even in dealing with the topographical connections of the legends we have to proceed with great caution, inasmuch as certain places may have been called after characters in the stories. Families, too, in their emigrations, in accordance with the methods of emigrants everywhere, may have renamed certain places after places in their old homes, and legends themselves with their associated names often travel far afield.

The existence of the poems with which we are now dealing in their present form shows that they have a literary history behind them: they have recognized metres, a recognized poetic vocabulary and a sense of taste and style, and the more they are understood the more vividly do they reflect the ideals and interests which guided the minds of the Welsh people when Europe was emerging from the night of barbarism.

Note

The verses called 'Englynion y Beddau', which have affinities with the traditions and legends of several districts, also belong to the poetry of reflective meditation over the past. They are probably a development from a smaller nucleus. In the topographical elucidation of the old legends they are of real service.

www.ingramcontent.com/pod-product-compliance
Lightning Source LLC
Chambersburg PA
CBHW051555010526
44118CB00022B/2716